Scar and Flower

Also by Lee Herrick

This Many Miles from Desire
Gardening Secrets of the Dead
The World I Leave You: Asian American Poets on Faith and Spirit, co-editors
    Lee Herrick and Leah Silvieus (February 2020)

Scar and Flower

Lee Herrick

Word Poetry

Published by Word Poetry
P.O. Box 541106
Cincinnati, OH 45254-1106

ISBN: 9781625492944

Poetry Editor: Kevin Walzer
Business Editor: Lori Jareo

Cover photo by Christine H. Lee
Cover design by Lisa Lee Herrick
Author photo by Curtis Messer

Visit us on the web at www.wordpoetrybooks.com

Acknowledgments

The author expresses his gratitude to the editors of the following publications, where versions of these poems previously appeared:

Columbia Poetry Review, "Fatigue"

Gramma Poetry Daily, "What I Hear When I Hear You in My Head," "What I Hear After the Massacre and What I Mistake For My Heart," and "Flight"

Hyphen, "Echolocation," "Repertoire," and "Sun"

Lantern Review, "The House is Quiet, Except"

Leaf by Leaf, "Stars" and "Lecture"

Penumbra, "Manifesto" and "Dear ____,"

Spectrum, "Strawberries"

Taos International Journal of Poetry and Art, "Truths"

The Normal School, "Rose"

Table of Contents

I.   Scar

What we allow the mark of our suffering to become is in our own hands.

— bell hooks, *All About Love: New Visions*

Dear_____,

When you lost me, or when your heart caved,
or when your heart flew through the city like wild herons
on the ledge of my broken window sill in another country,
you named infinity as the home of your intoxication,
ferment as placeholder for love, the ocean sized grace
of our common language, the ocean sized chance in this
moment. Grace. That's what I meant to tell you about.
I saw it a few times in my life. I saw my daughter cradle
the broken body of a tiny bird. I saw a young poet
repair the broken charm of a younger poet. I saw that
poet forgive another poet by a stream in the City of God,
by a monument for mothers like you who write poems
about men like me, who write by the ocean with their dogs
waking in the morning cool, the wild seabirds searching
the waves for a small fish to devour.

What I Hear After the Massacre and What I Mistake For My Heart

After Newtown

Invisible birds shocked out of the trees
and you mistake them for children
on the playground, or you mistake the leaves
cracked underfoot for the children's hush
or broken glass. It's a maelstrom.
At the Winter Program, the first graders
sing "Let It Snow" and the parents clasp
their hands, half exhale, half prayer.
The children sing in your town and you
think of the children in the shattered town.
All that comes to you is their hearts, heaven,
hell, and the next kind word you will say to a boy.

What I Hear When I Hear You in My Head

is the little whisper, the aggregate sorrow, the father's
heavy weeping as the son's heavy weeping. What I hear
is your artistic response after the massacre, the family
of clasped hands, Black hands, Brown hands, a small child
whose brother never had a chance, who holds her father's
tearful face and says, "Your eyes are like the moon," is
what I hear when I hear you in my head this evening,
your laughter like tiny harps. I hear your fatigue as
another way to say: deprivation. I hear recount, re-tally,
a retaliation is what I hear when I hear you in my head
is the grace, the charm, the dead, the boy, the dead boy,
the boy who died because of the fear, the forest
in the other man's heart, the gun, the heartbreak
is the sound I hear when I hear you in my head
is how we each sigh with distinction, where
fatigue meets fire, where we wake and wonder:
if we all go out to a field tonight, sit by a fire,
say the most honest thing you have ever said in your life,
would any dead boy or girl reappear, not like a mirage
but reappear, not like a voice in my head but a body
in this room, with flesh and bones, with his big smile,
orange blossoms in his billowing hair?

What I Hear When I Begin to Lose My Vision

A boy whose first sight may have been
an ajumma, pastor, or cop, or a street kid
praying for better weather. I grew up as if aging
was my right, as if when you read a poem in front
of a crowd and your vision fails you, they care
like they care for the words in the poem they have
not yet heard. I have read so many letters, from
a woman who wrote sarang hae, sarang hae,
in fine point cursive. This was after my big failures.
Before my vision became a tired song and I read
about sound because I wanted to know what last
part of the city I would know: when we die, we go
out into a field of lights or a lit cloud or a final apology
or a deep hum in your mother's private language.
If you ever come back from the dead, I hear that
all the senses go: no sight, no smell, no feel, no taste.
But you can hear. The doctor peels off her surgical
gloves and exhales. A nurse states the time of death:
7:25. Down the hall and outside the room, you
hear a woman, perhaps a mother or aunt, say
she had a boy. It's a miracle. *She had a boy.*

I Got a Letter from the Government the Other Day

I watched my hands turn into flags,
waving at the top of a government building before the bombs,
I watched books about fat content burn on the crosswalk
where a dead pigeon splayed out like a Banksy
where the drunk poets walked to the café
to haggle over Whitman's place in the canon
this is so far from any large scale weaponry
most kids could care less about revolution or poetry
but revolution has everything to do with the fire
lit in the girl whose father read to her
so that when she is fully grown and the bombs
detonate on her city's bridges she will know
the perfect epigraph to rally the women
who know where the wood and the matches await.

Fatigue

The mother cries into her black tea.
The mother weeds in the small yard.

The father cries into his old tea,
tries to bring his son back to life, wonders

why again, why the gun, why the cop,
why the fire, where's the rain,

why the gun, why the gun,
why the hole, in the head, in the dream

why theater, why the school grounds,
why headline, why sonnet,

why ammunition, why the acquittal,
why the killer can't hear the doves

why the boy cannot run with a hood
why some men craft hate with theirs

why again, why the gun, why the cop
where's the out, where's the cry

why the tie, why the tale,
why the black, why the brown,

why again, why we die,
why the sun go down like this.

Rose

At the New York Botanical Garden, for Orlando

This sudden desire to bloom, near
the astonishing splendor of the swamp,
there you are, unexpected and delivered
grace, rose and botany, petal and lure.
When the tourists leave, tell me
if you get tired. Why are you the Queen?
In another country, you are not royalty.
Tell me, rose, about root, soil, wilt.
I'm stealing a petal, and I know it's a crime.
I want the petal to fly from this botanical
garden to Orlando, where I cannot place a rose
on any altar but where I imagine forty-nine roses
near a swamp in a park where even small children
know, *don't terrorize the birds!* Let no person deliver
terror in a park, in a school, in a dance club, no
terror in a dance club. I want to be quiet.
The roses admit they don't know why they bloom.
But they do. The rose, its pulse, doing its loveliness
in a time of disaster, dancing like the world was on fire.

Survival

I did not hold the gun
that killed the twelve year old brother.
I do not have a brother, and I do not believe in armor.
When you speak of that day you speak about a strike
of lightning, the impossible wave of grief, after
the deer was killed and forever became a question.
You can spend decades searching for
a church with enough pews
a field with enough acreage
a band with enough rage
no amount of volume
quiets a sound like this
when we say death we mean
the final angel out of the gate
when we say grief we mean
buried and gasp every so often
at your own surprise how you find
enough acreage in the long poem, enough
pews in the ode, enough rage in the villanelle,
and you ride those forms until the moon begins
to speak to you in a language you can't even remember.

Repertoire

The nastiest lick in the whole damn repertoire
is in the first movement, the conductor said
to the first violin. A concerto like tonight's is
a dream swell, a dark circus of fluted magic,
the nasty hell of your own difficult year,
the bright chorus of your own survival, awash
in a floral weave of ocean foam among the dreaming
musicians preparing for the nasty lick, their lips
tightened like fists, rusted knives in a deep inventory:
one blade for large game, one blade for short trees,
one blade for berries, one blade for gutting the whole
damn idea. We have, what the conductor would call
a repertoire: how to maneuver if you aren't in tune,
how to bail when the wave overtakes you, when
the concerto has such mean licks you almost break,
the lights dizzy the fighter in you, but your repertoire
comes back to you in some animal moment, your breath
now in time with your instrument, and everything
aligns as it should: your glistening body healed from
the incision, your flawed key buried under your shining
knives, your favorite chapter, your go to song.

Exile

Our natural state
is not

defensive
or tense

but water
in a resting

state.
We state this

to be true
in an age

of inquiry,
our failure

to put what
is just

before
ease. There

are lovers in
another country

reclining by
a fire, admitting

love in
a common language

with faith
in the exiles

of their state,
where

a woman
looks at her friend

and says
please, put down

your bag
and stay.

Please, stay
to see how

the movie ends.
Take my hand.

I think the city
might go

up
in flames.

Translation

A murder in the empty field, a murder
in the busy dream, a murder in the long
driveway where lovers yield to the quieter
deaths of the tired leaves. In the odd language
of my dreams, there is no word for massacre,
no two consecutive words to mean school
shooting, no direct translation for stage four
or sui generis, but there's always a murder
in the empty field, a murder in the busy dream
when we thought our mind was the quiet beach
but we come to know there is no quiet place
but shotguns, hysterical parents, chants
in the language of each country's peasantry
gathered elegance in the plaza.

Wildfire

The wild fire,
all energy and devour,

the fire's wild intention--
char, shatter, engulf.

It was nature
on nature,

lightning on sequoia,
disaster

like man strikes woman
or the sick

alchemy of wound
and kill,

wound
the child and he

might kill
one of his own,

or one
of your own,

then go
after the trees,

after
the immigrants,

the oceans,
after

any damned
thing he can destroy.

Stray Light

Oh Lady Mercy,
our country of auction block

and cracked teeth
under the steel toed boot,

how easy our dismissal
because the game is on.

Say the robots
learned to love

by the time I discovered my body,
fireflies organized

the stray light,
harnessed it for energy

in small villages
for dreaming women.

The men listened
to the elders report by the fire light:

if you gather the data
from your heartbreak

you'll find it's just dust now.
It is not too late for discovery.

It is not too late to learn the radius
of past despair.

The children forget
about maps,

never knew they existed,
so they lost the art of getting lost,

of being
lost, of feeling loss.

If it were only shock,
the after shock of your spine tremble,

if it were only about waves: water,
electrical, sound, the slow rumble

you know by now,
we would walk around

with our dumb mouths
open in awe,

not because we are dumb
but because a father cradles a dying

stranger with his left leg gone,
with metal shrapnel peppered

into the side of his face, near
his cheekbones, where the stranger,

a boy, touches the man's
face and learns the importance

of human touch
in the minutes before dying.

Testimony

I heard the American poet groan
like his farmworker mother bent
into California's central question
like a rake or a comma or a death
that was not a death but a rising
fire or a shotgun in a wheat field.

I heard the father say to himself
to hell with it before he wrote
a seven page manifesto on the crimes
of lemon trees whose leaves become
little whispers in our dream like
yellow flowers floating on a lake.

I heard anger come into the night
I heard the night bring you down
I heard the down say please madam
I heard a woman say Hmong means free
I heard freedom like kingdom.

Prize

Little star of the ancient, teeming city
your body is a torrent, a current, apology
and punishment, lit up in the sky, a prize:
best in show for the boffant poodle
crazed and prancing like a stoned deer,
his eyes locked on the year's supply of treats.
I saw the little star, a writer, frothing
at the mouth once. It was July, and the judges
were all from the South and the winner had
a particular drawl: rather perfect given the writer's
habit of slurring the story's key repeating words:
machine gun, blood bath, elegy. But it was a well
told story. When kids this young die in a massacre,
don't judge the teacher who tried to save lives.
If you don't know what to make of her, read the part
of the story again where she huddles together
with the children and prays for her terror to make
no sound. Forget about prizes, apologies and desires.
Place her in the center of the action and let her speak,
her wild howl in the canyon full of trees.

Flags

Imagine how they fly or burn,
abandon

the canopy
of our modern resistance.

What happened to your patriots?
When my heart broke,

tiny clouds
poured into my hands

then turned into more tiny hearts —
cut the hair

from my body
and prepare me for your story,

your aunt's blood
into the river,

your mother's face
you cannot remember,

your father's ghost voice,
chasing

the burning
flags into the fire.

Cherubs

If guns speak a language
the birds comprehend,

then the dead conjure angels
in their free time, cherubs

with parachutes, heavy
metals and guns

painted to mirror
the local flora, the bomb

full of bluster and kill,
a Hello Kitty sticker

on the soldier's
busted helmet to remind

him of his daughter's
favorite colors.

Butterfly

What could be more foolish than dreaming of a butterfly
as you are shot while singing your country's anthem,
dreaming of your storefront lined with hungry patrons
who made you a millionaire, waking each morning
with a beautiful woman near you, a small patch of grass
to water, to keep slightly green, to grow flowers around
as if to prepare for some dead in this foolish idea
where everyone survives their traumatic entry wounds
and there is enough blood and technique to save the bleeding,
the fierce and the brave, portraits of ferocity
but they don't have guns, but let's say they begin to dream
too, and let's say each bullet has a tiny poem inscribed on it,
the sonnet on copper tearing through the country's heat,
where the world ends but thank God for the waking.

Firefly

I wrote her name in the sand
with the tiny parade of fireflies

flitting above my head
and it came true,

a nearly black night
lit with bright yellow question

marks, little fires
you thought would break you

but never did, not even
the long year of paralysis.

When you write your
daughter's name in the sand

it is permanent, even as the water
washes it away, you

have done it — that was the act,
the action, permanent as fire.

Wildflowers

I asked the florist
for a batch of wildflowers and ran in your

direction, I lost my shirt and let
my skin be in the wind, the dolphins,

sleek like me, but as for us, the irresistible
sea is to separate us. As for an hour

carrying us, what is the worst that could
come from a light stroll on the beach?

The florist handed me the batch of seagrass.
I paint moons by the ocean because dying

in an asylum is difficult to paint.
What good is a year without ambition,

without fire to char the skin of your animal engine,
without apology to correct history's wandering plot.

The natives farm the berries and will own it all,
after all. What I mean to say is, we could wander

out to find our own beach with no boundaries,
bonfires every time the sun goes down.

Revolution

The revolution broke out
in your very own heart.
Your heart a hundred
flaming questions.
The daughters' strong
arms, a bounty, a blue sky
melting down every semi-
automatic. What guns ever
eased a grandmother's trauma?
The revolution broke out in riots.
It was all women and girls.
They taught me how to say guerra.
She said the city is in my heart.
She said Oaxaca, Chiapas,
Teotihuacan. Chichicastenango,
Tegucigalpa, San Salvador.
She said my name is Hue, Seoul,
Qingdao. Guangzhou. Luong
Prabang, Phnom Penh,
Kingston, Chiang Mai,
Mumbai, Manila, Havana,
Tehran, Shiraz, Mosul,

Fallujah, Mukalla, Rafah,
Mogadishu, Kyoto, Aleppo,
Fresno. The girl on fire inside
my heart said don't forget the woman's
hands, the arms, her ocean sized
heart, aunt's molcajete,
her sister's papaya salad.
She said, measure the capacity
of your chest, what valves
and caves to excavate.
She said, tonight, let us
do what the heart teaches
us, how it breaks us open
and shakes us clean.
Protect it. How the world
is a story——the afternoon
sunlight in a girl's black hair,
the fine lines in a woman's
small hands, the dreams
they share by the fire.

Waking

For the bullet spun in the grown
man's fingers, at home, at rest,
before he decides, before the decision
he thinks irrevocable, maybe the bullet
has already left the gun, maybe the word
has already left your mouth, words cannot
re-enter the mouth, so maybe in the end
we are violent, we must violate, we must
assault the quiet air with our own careless
thrashing, the word, the chemical,
the profane battery, the quiet bookshelf
full of first editions, what do we lose
when we talk about power, what do we forget
when we remember our names, our children's
names, the loud dead names crashing
about in the study?

If I Held You

like a book, considered dialogue
and plot development

while I read you,
would we know if we'd fallen?

When holding a book,
our hands like prayer

or an open rose,
forgiveness

at the halfway point.
When we meant

to turn every page
with more care

more awareness of the sound
of a caregiver

on her knees
whispering to infants

her idea of farewell,
her hands in the shape of a chapel

everyone's head down
everyone's dream held in a page.

Erasure

When I was boy and the moon
had not yet occurred to me, my name
given to me by an American couple full of grief
and readiness, I sinned by cursing my mother.
How could I know I would need the moon?
I wished bad things for her because she cared
hard that I would make it. I cursed her because
I knew the shape of her hand, a porcelain shell
lighter than mine, and I could not form the words
to curse anyone else. Every now and then,
I remember that I was born on the other side
of the world, and it makes sense that I love
looking at the stars, such a foolish thing to do
as a grown man, my brown body glistening
in the pool, starlight flashing in my wet black hair.

Elegy

For Phillip Clay (1974-2017) - born in South Korea adopted
to the United States, deported back to Korea, committed
suicide in 2017

In my dream, when you fell through
the sky from fourteen stories high,
all burning paper, your body broke
into a hundred flowers and floated
into the clouds. The moon and stars: still.
Your fire now ash, your spirit free, wild,
and true in a deep calm where country
is a black night, a blank question
of insufficient starlight, where no child,
man or woman, no idea as beautiful as you
is ever deported, is ever only the harsh light
of your deepest wound. I wish I could have
eaten your fire and howled with you:
eclipse, fracture, angelic cloud song.
May the wild and broken stars remember you.
May you be at peace in a quiet part of the sky.

How Music Stays in the Body

Your body is a song called birth
or first mother, a miracle that gave birth
to another exquisite song. One song raises
three boys with a white husband. One song
fought an American war overseas. One song leapt
from fourteen stories high, and like a dead bird,
shattered into the clouds. Most forgot the lyrics
to their own bodies or decided to paint abstracts
of mountains or moons in the shape of your face.
I've been told Mothers don't forget the body.
I can't remember your face, the shape or story,
or how you held me the day I was born, so
I wrote one thousand poems to survive.
I want to sing with you in an open field,
a simple room, or a quiet bar. I want to hear
your opinions about angels. Truth is, angels drink,
too—soju spilled on the halo, white wings sticky
with gin, as if any mother could forget the music
that left her. You should hear how loudly I sing
now. I've become a ballad of wild dreams and coping
mechanisms. I can breathe now through any fire.
I imagine I got this from him or you, my earthly
inheritance: your arms, your sigh, your heavy song.

I know all the lyrics. I know all the blood.
I know why angels howl into the moonlight.

Manifesto

I wanted to write a manifesto
about the ocean,

a treatise on the wild trees'
outlandish demands,

alone under moonlight
translating my name:

dreamer, ascendant,
question.

My Korean name
means bright light,

what appears after
despair,

how you write Korean
instead of Koran

and think
of your friend

who worked Gibran
into his wedding

vows, how
love is the water

between two beaches,
one a country

where your name was
Lee Kwang Soo,

one a country
where you are renamed

Lee Herrick, and you are
what you always

were, a question,
a bruised persimmon,

a dreamer
imagining the revolt.

Breath

1.

By the time I discovered my body
it was perfectly human, all this sin,
the chambers and aorta of the large muscle,
I was a series of numbers on a chart,
the start of the mouth

2.

If you gather the data
from the robots of your city
the wires all shine
in certain light and the kids
inhale a canopy of polluted air
heave a last prayer

3.

We call the body, heart
calls the body, the body calls the hurt
natural, we call nature a tree on fire
from only heat, its own burn

4.

We call this idea: agriculture,
poetry culture
or office culture:
the sum, the atoms. What you take
in before you let breath out.

Lecture

I came to hear the painter
talk about sunlight

in Paris but herons broke out
of the tiny lecture hall.

The painter caught one
with her bare hand

as it sprung. This,
she claimed, was joyful

equal to anything
she could say

about the influence of light
in Lima on her work.

We felt the light
in the room like the light

in the herons' pale feathers
that became the painters'

dark pastels, the bruises
of her next wild idea.

II.   Flower

The earth laughs in flowers.

—Ralph Waldo Emerson

A bit of fragrance clings to the hand that gives flowers.

—Chinese Proverb

Flight

The in-flight magazine crossword partially done,
a corner begun here, scratched out answers there,
one set of answers in pencil, another in the green.
The woman with the green ball point knew
the all-time hit king is Rose and the Siem Reap
treasure is Angkor Wat. The woman, perhaps
en route to hold her dying mother's hand in Seattle,
forgot about death for ten minutes while remembering
her husband's Cincinnati Reds hat while gardening after
the diagnosis. Her handwriting was so clean. Maybe
she was a surgeon. Maybe a painter. No. What painter
wouldn't know 17-down, Diego's love, five letters?
In a rush, her dying mother's voice came back
to her, or maybe she was a Chinese adoptee
and her first mother's imagined voice said, wo ai ni.
At 30,000 feet, you focus on 33-across, Asian
American classic, *The Woman* _____,
when a stranger in the window seat sees the clue,
watches me write in W, and she says *Warrior.*
and for a moment you forget it is your favorite memoir,
and she reminds you of lilies or roses, Van Gogh
or stems with thorns, art galleries in romantic cities

where she is headed but you should not go. The flight
attendant grazes my shoulder. The crossword squares,
the letters, the chairs and aisles seem so tight in flight,
but there is nothing here but room, really.
Maybe the next passenger will know
what I do not: 64-down, five letters, Purpose.
And why do we remember what we do? We know
the buzz of Dickinson's fly and the number of years
in Marquez's solitude, but some things we will never
know, as it should be: why the body sometimes rumbles
like a plane hurtling over southern Oregon, how
exactly we fall in love, or if Frida and Maxine
Hong Kingston would have loved the same kind of tea.

Echolocation

What a miracle it would be
to echolocate like a bat,

to shriek and have the shriek
bounce back to alert us

to the oncoming train, the wrong person,
or a year of trouble.

The organism which hears best
is the Greater Wax Moth,

which can hear 100 kHz more
than the bat, which preys on the moth.

And what do we hear, with poor night
vision and no ability for flight?

Can you hear your lover hum near the stove?
You are one of many species who can whistle.

Pigeons hear lower frequencies
and can detect coming storms.

Dogs can differentiate between their owners'
footsteps and a stranger's.

And what have you heard tonight,
the low sigh of your father's fatigue,

the scrape of a brush on the canvas,
the echo of your singular breathing.

Truths

"Some things you know all your life. They are so simple and
true, they must be said without elegance."
— Philip Levine

I will say it like this: I watched my daughter bite into a peach,
and although she did not have the language for it yet,
I imagined her thinking, that taste, that perfect juice,
is heavenly. There was a certain light in Fresno that day,
like today, where we work and dream—
Mayor and mothers, farmers and fathers, laborers
in blue collars and donors for the red wave,
one city of multiple truths straight down the 99
dreaming about the perfect peach, the perfect pitch,
one city in the shape of an immigrant's beautiful accent,
one city of taco, gyro, pan dulce, and strawberries
so good, you'd swear they came straight from the hand of God,
one city, in my dream, where there are no gunshots tonight
or the next one hundred starlit nights, one simple truth
called the fig tree, the ash tree, one poet's testimony
stripped of its elegance for the city to consider:
in which of our ninety languages should I say that I love you?
Which of our two hundred and fifty different crops would you like

to taste, to imagine its perfect juice? My truths involve dreams,
stars, hard work and good pay for the ice worker, the tractor
driver, the backyard gardener, the students and the teachers,
the nurses and the preachers. The fog on a country road—
that is the truth. Our menacing heat in July—truth.
My city is your city, a bead of sweat and the will
to work, the want for clean air, for water,
for a moment of grace in the shade.

Strawberries

I pulled into the dirt lot for delicious strawberry
because I stop for entrepreneurs and grammar like that.
What is more American? I too came from another country,
like someone once did in your family, who had what it took
to farm in a new language, learn the laws, learn the people.
When I was a boy before I became a citizen,
I pledged allegiance to the flag before I knew
what allegiance was, what an ally was, what a republic was,
or what it meant to stand. I entered the dream of the farmer
when I walked up to his business, each basket
of berries another dollar for his son who has not been
to Southeast Asia but knows California well, knows
the supermarkets and the malls, the ocean swells
and the angle of sunlight in his mother's fatigue.
The farmer speaks like a poet, dreaming about the river
back home. I bet his favorite American poet would be Rich
or Whitman, Espada or Vang. I buy six baskets and no sky opens,
no doves break into flight but the first perfect strawberry
glistens in the valley light before I take it into my mouth
and become a citizen of these open American fields.

Happiness

for Juan Felipe Herrera

American Poets magazine: How do you see poetry enriching American
life and culture?

Juan Felipe Herrera: With a sense of a new happiness—[as] we float
through the new, ever-evolving technologies and the crazy, painful
gaps of class, culture, and power.

For the fire, for the hands, for the dust sifted through
all the book spines, the poems sprouted like cilantro
for a young Juanito who posed in the Greyhound photo
booth and words began to dance, where a new happiness
took root in the sprawling constellation of a city, where
in the morning light of Fresno or El Paso, Escondido
or San Diego, a girl hears a Juan Felipe Herrera poem
and imagines herself in flight, her own outer space:
the astronomy of the maestro's language like glow-
in-the-dark stars taped to her ceiling, the galaxy
of his poems like estrellas of her dreams.

What I mean to say is: love. Teenage poets with moonlight

in their hair, elders from your neighborhood who know
he's the real deal: did I mention Flor y Canto in 1973?
He said, let us gather in a flourishing way, something
like doves in flight or a super cilantro girl who saves
the day, like farm workers with accents like perfect chiles.

You said once that the art of writing is the art of flying
and so you teach us to dismantle our heavy wings.
You are something like the sun—the equivalent in size
of one million earths, what light you have, what fire
you give, what joy grows from your wild astronomy
in bright dazzle lighting these very skies.

Prayers

Imagine you are
the last line in this
poem somewhere
in a desert with no
data or comment
threads, only the creek
water light as a cloud,
in the sand
where plants quit.
You will wait
for the information:
map, verdict, prayer,
so be grateful, lovers,
be kind, children,
and the whole blanket
of stars will shake
out and settle like
tiny silver prayers
in your hair.

Anechoic

George Foy stayed in the anechoic chamber
for 45 minutes and nearly went mad.
He could hear the blood rushing in
his veins and began to wonder if he was
hallucinating. He had been to a monastery,
an American Indian sweat lodge,
and a nickel mine two kilometers underground.
In the anechoic chamber, the floor's design
eliminates the sound of footsteps.
NASA trains astronauts in anechoic chambers
to cope with the silence of space.
Without echo, in the quietest place on earth,
what else can we hold onto? What replaces sound
in concert with what you see? The human voice,
the timbre when a person says kamsahamnida
or yes, please, or fuerte, is 25 to 35 decibels.
Hearing damage can start around 115 decibels.
Metallica, front row, possible damage
albeit possible love. The Who, 126 decibels.
A Boeing Jet, 165 decibels. The whale, low rumble
frequency and all, 188 decibels, can be heard
for hundreds of miles underwater.

I once walked around inside a whale heart,
which is the size of a small car. The sound
was like Brian Doyle's heart that gave out
at 60 after he wrote my favorite essay
about the joyas voladoras and the hummingbird
heart, the whale heart, and the human
heart. Glass can break at 163 decibels.
Hearing is the last sense to leave us.
Some say that upon death, our vision,
our taste, our touch, and our smell
might leave us, but some have been
pronounced dead and by all indication
are, but they can hear. In this moment,
when the doctor pronounces the time
or when the handgun pumps once more,
what light arrives? What sounds, the angels?
The Ultrasonic Weapon is used for crowd control
or to combat riots—as too many
humans gathered in one place for a unified
purpose can threaten the state. The state
permits gatherings if the flag waves. Sound
can be weaponized or made into art.
It can kill. It can heal a wound. It is
a navigation device and can help determine
if the woman has a second heart inside of her

now, the beating heart of a baby on the ultrasound,
a boy or a girl, making a new music in the body
of another body, a chorus, a concert, a hush.

Sun

> The sun, with all those planets revolving around it and
> dependent on it, can still ripen a bunch of grapes as if it had
> nothing else in the universe to do.
>
> —Galileo

When I was a boy, and the moon had not yet occurred to me,

the astronomy of my body was simple and true.

I was all sun, all heat, all brown adoption high on fire.

I got lost in a forest I thought was an ocean.

My sister knew it was a lake but let me figure it out.

I saw the lilies, the dying, the heartbreak to come.

So I came to the idea that I would not die

before I spent a full night staring up at the moon

before I wrote a poem near Teohotihuacan,

before I returned to the city in which I became an erasure /

before the other side of planet becomes home,

the California poppies in the front yard, the grape

vines in full regalia with their questions

exploding right there on the branch.

Park

One afternoon,
full moon

and all, my friend's
older brother

put a gun
in his mouth,

the copper metal
alloy shattered

the head
in an instant,

one son
gone

into the denouement,
startled

from the echo
of a gun

shot in a quiet
California park,

rum stains
on the wooden bench

where fading
pocketknife art says

I was here. How
do we know

who was here?
What cloud

ever keeps its form?
What knife, gun,

or cloud
even matters compared

to the ways
I've imagined your smile?

What old life
do I hope for

you, daughter?
Why those chemicals

haywire in the brain?
Where should I place

my altar
of prayers

before they begin
to rust,

decompose,
and fall apart?

Stay

I am not what you thought
an ocean would look like,
but once a fire starts in you,
there will always be ash.
There are long walks, thank
goodness, there are woods
to be small in, there are
anchors to the world so
you will not fly away before
it is time. The miracle of grass,
even though you may forget it,
the fact that you are loved,
even though you may forget it,
and what a miracle that is—
being loved—or more so,
that you are a wide blue ocean
capable of loving, you churning
body of sea life who survived
the oil spills, the broken glass,
the dead birds floating in the bay.

Pigeon

It was regal and arrogant,
so pronounced and bright,
the rain so clean. Then the storm,
then the death. I thought of the pigeons
in Peru in late winter
when everything began to fail, even
my ability to watch the birds.
But this California pigeon,
a moon queen. July, storm.
It rubbed its grey head
against the wet window,
put its head down as if
to surrender, as if to say
if the lightning comes and
I am nowhere near shelter,
I will remember what electricity
conducts: enough voltage to kill
a man or woman dead on the spot.
It threw its head back and took
the lightning that I did not see,
although I heard the thing
spit out a last breath, and I sat

in my chair and watched the whole death
go down, the life gone quiet just like that.

Discipline

In the woods, the campfire
goes out,

you lace up
and go

for a run
on the one smooth path,

the fireflies
splayed

against the stars,

the hot
jasmine tea ready.

For the eighth
straight dream,

it was a night
of sweating

out the fire
from your life,

how light
began to flash,

how your discipline
sounded

like Korean mothers
yelling,

smelled of
firewood or ash.

Decomposition

My country fell apart.
What I mean to say is:

we forgot about the stars.
We forgot we need the moon.

We asked all the wrong questions
about our founding documents,

all burnt wire and fray.
We focused on the bullets

and the outcry instead
of the corporation and the electorate

who make the bullets and the outcry.
Or the shining decor on the breastplate.

We complicated it all.
We were flattened with options.

We forgot our own fabric,
the miracles in our simple hands.

Survival

What is that moment in evening light
when everything softens,

the word for
all the city's trouble

welled around us,
the sparkle of your grandmother's

necklace? I was lost
once as you were, but we found

the starlight and waking
dreams of our bodies,

sure by the sounds
we echo

after all this trauma,
all this grace.

Hour

of that simple year,
of that easy charm

down by the beach
 front cottage, warm

bread from the oven
and you in the water

from that large grace,
from that large stove

bought with our first
good idea, a love song.

Muse

You creature and muse
up in the tree, tiny ghost story

of yellow petals,
little histories of my ordinary laughter,

my lakes, my cities
on the hill my Jewish professor

dreamt of
you creature

of soft features
in the setting light,

in the evening spell
of fireflies and ease,

forgetting and black flies,
you fire,

you mirror in the river,
you burn

and burn,
and you almost burn out.

Midnight

Don't the soft lips
come with the throat
of a sparrow,

spangled and narrow
enough to snap
with your two

weak fingers?
Don't they get wet
by the tongue

or the touch
of the singer's microphone
hand? If you touch

the arm or the hand,
little choruses
inside wake on

the romantic top floor
overlooking

the city's teeming youth,
the looming avalanche.

Bathe

Some acts require
the whole body's attention,

how a light song fills
the auditorium.

Little bath wave over arm,
kite over wine,

on your back
in a porcelain heart.

Tiny flowers
near your head so moist

you could almost live there,
the city crashing

around your hips,
the artists remembering

the maps
to their deep root,

all the ache washed
out,

all the wine
slipping down the throat.

Advice

When asked
why your last name does not sound Korean
and you have finished the internal sigh,

ask back, simply,
if they know Korea on a map
or can pronounce the word fatigue

in more than one language
ask back, simply,
if they hear comfort women

speak near the clouds,
militarized borders between
countries still at war

try, simply,
what trauma the child can name
as an adult

how what nearly killed you
is none of my business
or is all of my business

how I can do things
with names and this language
you cannot begin to fathom.

Morning

My daughter dreamed one morning
about a plate of scrambled eggs with a side
of aphorisms and we ate them.

I read her a poem
shaped like a thick pillar
in which the young speaker hit a young girl,

and she waited for the girl to hit her back,
to make it right. My daughter drew
a picture of three girls in fancy dresses

sitting on a couch. To the left of the couch,
a globe. To the right, a lamp. Above the girls,
a bookshelf with three books: one on poetry,

one on prose, and one on fairies.
I could lie in this poem and tell you
the immeasurable peace I felt that morning

had something to do with history and the future
both perfectly distant so that
all the world's music converged in our kitchen.

But I wanted to teach my daughter how to punch
someone, how in the midst of the gracious
civility we teach her, there may be a time

that I hope never comes, but if it is between
her and a horrible violence against her,
I hope she will know how to make a fist,

or she will know what words to unveil,
what lightning to throw, how to break
a man's nose and make it bleed.

Stars

Every now and then, I remember I was born

on the other side of the world, and it makes sense

that I love looking at the stars:

Little Apocalypse, The Human Condition,

The Bell Tribe, clusters I invent above the field

where I kissed a woman with hair like black gold.

When Van Gogh looked out his asylum room

window and painted "Starry Night," the stars

above his country went blank for an instant—you

wouldn't have noticed—his hands all flurry and oils,

energy and devour, like fire, here a moon

with feathery wings, there a spangled crush of cloud.

In his eyes, the stars like madness.

In the stars, your country and silver shots of light.

In the window, your best self, your supernova,

your midnight prayer against dying.

The House is Quiet, Except

my daughter reads on the couch,
whispers the dialogue. I only hear

the consonants of her name, the way

I imagine a house of books
in a future age,

2035, when I will be 65 and alive,

I hope, and she will be 31,
perhaps with faith and a love

she can count on—wild trees,

wild flowers, a man, or a woman.
Perhaps God or someone else

to whom she can whisper dialogue
if she forgets where her heart is,

how there is a pulse in every book,

how looking down into the open page
reminds us of prayer,

the next night of restoration,
the light around her body.

Bio

Lee Herrick is the author of *Gardening Secrets of the Dead* (WordTech Editions, 2012) and *This Many Miles from Desire* (WordTech Editions, 2007). His poems have been published widely in literary magazines including *Berkeley Poetry Review, The Bloomsbury Review, Columbia Poetry Review, The Normal School, The Poetry Foundation,* and *ZZYZYVA*; literary anthologies including *Highway 99: A Literary Journey Through California's Great Central Valley*, 2nd edition, *The Place That Inhabits Us: Poems from the San Francisco Bay Watershed, One for the Money: The Sentence as Poetic Form,* and *Indivisible: Poems of Social Justice*; his prose appears in the college textbooks *Visions Across the Americas*, 8th edition, *The Writer's Workplace,* and *Interactions*. He was born in Daejeon, South Korea, adopted at ten months old, and lives with his wife and daughter in Fresno, California. He served as Fresno Poet Laureate from 2015-2017 and is on the Advisory Board of The Adoption Museum Project. He teaches at Fresno City College and in the MFA Program at Sierra Nevada College.

CPSIA information can be obtained
at www.ICGtesting.com
Printed in the USA
FSHW010948130319
56335FS